Work it!

a modern-day sales planner

BY TANIA ARAKELIAN DOUB

ZERO TO QUOTA **in 9 0 DAYS**

Tania Arakelian Doub is also the author of *Work It, Girl! A modern-day career guide for women in sales*. The companion to this sales planner, *Work It, Girl!*, is the essential handbook for any modern-day woman navigating a career in technology sales. In her book, Tania compiles twenty years of her sales experience—job profiles, career trajectories, anecdotes, tips and tricks, and more—and has created *the* blueprint to a long and sustainable career for women in sales. Find it on www.Amazon.com or visit www.taniadoub.com.

CONNECT WITH ME

tania@taniadoub.com

www.taniadoub.com

LinkedIn.com/in/taniadoub

Work it! a modern-day sales planner

Contents

Introduction

Hello!

My name is Tania Arakelian Doub and, after twenty years of selling SaaS, I can't wait to share my powerful sales approach with you, that will produce impressive results! Let's face it. Sales is a bit of a roller coaster ride from one day to the next. And there is no formal blueprint on how to do this job. No classic sales training is offered at the majority of colleges across the country, but the majority of us find ourselves in sales at one point or another in our careers!

Work It! a modern-day sales planner, is about empowering you to confidently manage your day to day, so that you have the confidence and the energy to sustain a career in sales - without even questioning whether you even *belong* in sales. It's about giving you the framework - and the discipline - to create a sales process of your own that is sustainable and productive each and every day. And more importantly, following this process will help you eliminate distractions and focus precisely on what you need to do to crush your number from one quarter to the next.

Over the years, I have been searching for the perfect sales notebook. Something to help me capture my enthusiasm, energy and anxiety for my job - all in one place. Nothing even comes close to what I need to manage my day. Or my pipeline! [Nevermind my quota - but to also have my accounts, my notes, my action items, my progress and my focus - all in one place!] So, what's the deal? Am I actually suggesting a notebook is the only thing keeping you from crushing your number this quarter? **YES!** And after two decades in the field, the one tool that I rely on - and the one thing I know for sure - is that the best way to accomplish something - *anything*! - that you set out to do, is to actually write it down.

I have been following this exact format to give me the structure and discipline to do my job every day. If I'm being honest, when I take the time to be this disciplined, I crush my number every time. <u>When I cut corners, it's so much harder!</u>

So, go ahead. Work it!
Because you already have what it takes.

And now you have the notebook, too.

That's why I've created this portable, usable, and simple vision board for the sales profession-al – with you in mind! To be productive every month, every week, every day while you keep pipeline generation top of mind! Without ever feeling overwhelmed by it all.

Tania

My Notes

What are my big accounts this quarter?

1. _____

2. _____

3. _____

What tools or technologies do I need to better leverage at work?

1. _____

2. _____

3. _____

What people or resources do I need to better leverage at work?

1. _____

2. _____

3. _____

What whitepapers or collateral should I reference most often?

1. _____

2. _____

3. _____

Which dashboards does my manager look at each week?

_____

_____

_____

_____

Things I'm grateful for at work

_____

_____

_____

One new habit

_____

_____

_____

Articles

_____

_____

_____

Podcasts

_____

_____

_____

People to follow

_____

_____

_____

People to meet

_____

_____

_____

My Quarterly REVIEW

Date _____

Take a moment to reflect on your performance last quarter.

☐ President's Club, here I come!

☐ Keeping calm and making progress.

☐ If I'm being honest, I need a better plan.

Now, just get real with yourself. Did you crush it? Did you stay in your comfort zone because that was, well, comfortable? Did you lose sight of your goals? What momentum are you carrying into this quarter?

_____

_____

_____

_____

_____

_____

_____

_____

_____

_____

Work it! a modern-day sales planner

Pipeline Health

MY PLANNING WORKSHEET

Baby steps. You got this.

What's my target quota this year?   What's my target quota this quarter?

_____   _____

STEP 1: PIPELINE REVIEW

Look at your CRM. Record all your active deals and dollar amounts in your pipeline.

PRO TIP: This list does not have to match your CRM stages. Be honest on where things belong. The goal is to understand where you stand and where you need to focus.

This should be used as a private and honest conversation with yourself alone.

Account	Solid deal (commit)	Has potential (most likely)	Damn, it's just filler (long shot)
Total	$ Box 1	$ Box 2	$

Do you have a solid pipeline and see a path to your number?   ☐ Yes ☐ No

STEP 2: PIPELINE PULL FORWARD

Now take a look at next quarter.
Any potential for a pull forward? List out your top three deals.

Account	Dollar amount	Why does this have potential for a pull forward?
1.		
2.		
3.		
Total	$ Box 3	

STEP 3: PATH TO SUCCESS

Now let's do some math.

		Notes
Record your quarterly target quota HERE:	$	
Record your potential HERE: (Add totals for Box 1 + Box 2 + Box 3)	$	

Now do you have a solid path to your number?   ☐ Yes   ☐ No

STEP 4: HONEST REVIEW

Take a hard look in the mirror. What's the deal?

☐ I got this!

☐ I'll need all the stars to align, but I'll be OK.

☐ OMG. I need to get cranking!

I got this!

Awesome! You have a solid pipeline and plan to get there. Now you'll need to visualize this list of accounts every single day so that you can create momentum and movement that will get you to your goal. You will use Step 1 as the starting point again next quarter/month. Don't forget to keep prospecting to fill your pipeline.

I'll need all the stars to align, but I'll be OK.

Solid. While it's super exciting-and time consuming-to work deals in motion, dedicate time every single week to prospecting. You will thank yourself next quarter. Trust me! Same rules apply from above, too!

OMG. I need to get cranking!

Your pipeline needs to be 3X your quota. Start the quarter/month strong with major prospecting efforts to develop pipe. Don't stress. You got this. Use the prospecting worksheet at the beginning of each week to maximize your planning.

My Quota Calculator
At the beginning of the month, take a moment to calculate and record your quota so it's top of mind.

My ANNUAL quota:

_____

My QUARTERLY quota:

q1 _____
q2 _____
q3 _____
q4 _____

My quota THIS MONTH:

_____

Are you on a ramp quota? Does your quota vary by month? Write it out.

CLOSED/WON to date:

_____

Notes

Sunday	Monday	Tuesday

My quota this month is

Wednesday	Thursday	Friday	Saturday

My Target Accounts

Write down your target account list here. It can be the entire list, your focus for the quarter, or your Tier 1 accounts. Simply write them down in a way that allows you to group them together for more efficient prospecting. Either way, use it as a quick reference to help you get organized so that you can get clarity on the accounts you want to focus on each day.

My Target Accounts

My Focus THIS WEEK
3 STEPS TO MAKING MY QUOTA

1. Identify: What are my focus accounts for this week?
These can include net new prospects, accounts on life support, prospects that have gone dark or a recent discovery meeting that you desperately need to turn into pipeline.

1. _____
2. _____
3. _____
4. _____
5. _____

2. Action: What are my action items this week?
This is not your to-do list. These are tasks that will create real movement and generate action in your accounts. Is it sending a follow-up email or scheduling a follow-up meeting? Is it making an executive connection or mapping out a mutual close plan?

_____
_____
_____
_____
_____
_____

PRO TIP #1: Spread these action items out over the next five days.

PRO TIP #2: These are action items you can take into your 1:1 with your manager.

3. Reflect: What results do I need to manifest this week?
These are things that need to happen this week to feel good about your efforts. Which dashboards or activity metrics do you need to hit? What housekeeping tasks have you been assigned by your manager or team?

_____
_____
_____
_____
_____
_____

Work it! a modern-day sales planner

My Prospecting THIS WEEK
WORKSHEET

The hardest part about prospecting is finding the time. So now, let's make time. Record your *Target Prospects* for this week. Then look at the different types of *Prospecting Activity* you can engage in and pick the activity (or activities) you are going to dedicate time to this week. This exercise is not meant to replace your bulk outreach. Rather, it's the time you will dedicate to understanding your accounts and their business priorities.

PRO TIP #1: Don't cheat. You can repeat target prospects in the same week. But NEVER repeat the same combination in the same week!

PRO TIP #2: These are great action items and strategies you can take into your 1:1 with your SDR/BDR for your weekly planning session.

Sunday	Monday	Tuesday	Wednesday	Thursday	Friday	Saturday

Target Prospects	
Account	1
Account	2
Account	3
Account	4
Account	5

Prospecting Activity	
Research (web articles, executive interviews, press releases, annual report, etc.)	A
Organizational mapping (including any partners)	B
Draft call or email scripts	C
Schedule call or email blitz	D
Other	E

NOTES

_____

_____

_____

_____

_____

Su | M | Tu | W | Th | F | Sa

DAILY INTENTION

Date _____

My quota this month is _____

The non-negotiables for myself:

- ☐ Drink Water
- ☐ Move my body
- ☐ Be Awesome

Target prospect:

To make notable movement in my accounts, today I will: - List out activities from your weekly prospecting menu. - Act on the big things that will move the needle with your priority accounts.	At this time:
☐	
☐	
☐	
☐	
☐	
☐	
☐	
☐	
☐	
☐	
☐	
☐	
☐	
☐	
☐	
☐	
☐	
☐	
☐	
☐	
☐	
☐	

Work it! a modern-day sales planner

NOTES

Su M Tu W Th F Sa   *Date* _____

DAILY INTENTION

My quota this month is _____

The non-negotiables for myself:

☐ *Drink Water*
☐ *Move my body*
☐ *Be Awesome*

Target prospect:

To make notable movement in my accounts, today I will: - *List out activities from your weekly prospecting menu.* - *Act on the big things that will move the needle with your priority accounts.*	At this time:
☐	
☐	
☐	
☐	
☐	
☐	
☐	
☐	
☐	
☐	
☐	
☐	
☐	
☐	
☐	
☐	
☐	
☐	
☐	
☐	
☐	
☐	
☐	

NOTES

Su M Tu W Th F Sa

DAILY INTENTION

Date _____

My quota this month is _____

The non-negotiables for myself:

☐ *Drink Water*
☐ *Move my body*
☐ *Be Awesome*

Target prospect:

To make notable movement in my accounts, today I will: - *List out activities from your weekly prospecting menu.* - *Act on the big things that will move the needle with your priority accounts.*	At this time:
☐	
☐	
☐	
☐	
☐	
☐	
☐	
☐	
☐	
☐	
☐	
☐	
☐	
☐	
☐	
☐	
☐	
☐	
☐	
☐	
☐	
☐	

Work it! a modern-day sales planner

NOTES

Su M Tu W Th F Sa   Date _____

DAILY INTENTION

My quota this month is _____

The non-negotiables for myself:

- ☐ *Drink Water*
- ☐ *Move my body*
- ☐ *Be Awesome*

Target prospect:

To make notable movement in my accounts, today I will: - *List out activities from your weekly prospecting menu.* - *Act on the big things that will move the needle with your priority accounts.*	At this time:
☐	
☐	
☐	
☐	
☐	
☐	
☐	
☐	
☐	
☐	
☐	
☐	
☐	
☐	
☐	
☐	
☐	
☐	
☐	
☐	
☐	
☐	

Work it! a modern-day sales planner

NOTES

DAILY INTENTION

Date _____

My quota this month is _____

The non-negotiables for myself:

☐ *Drink Water*

☐ *Move my body*

☐ *Be Awesome*

Target prospect:

To make notable movement in my accounts, today I will: - *List out activities from your weekly prospecting menu.* - *Act on the big things that will move the needle with your priority accounts.*	At this time:
☐	
☐	
☐	
☐	
☐	
☐	
☐	
☐	
☐	
☐	
☐	
☐	
☐	
☐	
☐	
☐	
☐	
☐	
☐	
☐	
☐	
☐	

NOTES

Fri_YAY!
RECAP

+ **Your Peach**: What were you particularly proud of this week? Did you break into a new logo? Make a meaningful connection? Learn something new? Give a killer preso? Ink a deal? Write it down!

_____

_____

_____

_____

− **Your Pit**: Let's be real. Not everything goes as planned. What can you do better next week? Better time management? Did you skip a prospecting day? Not enought time to prepare for that important meeting? Write it down!

_____

_____

_____

_____

$ **Your Pipe**: Did you generate any new pipe this week? Are you close? What actions do you need to take to get your prospect or the awesome discovery call you had into your pipe? Before you forget, write it down as a starting point for your focus next week.

_____

_____

_____

_____

**Your Profile**: Let's look at the numbers.

Is your forecast up to date?	☐ Yes	☐ No	
Does your activity dashboard look good?	☐ Yes	☐ No	
Did you generate new pipeline this week?	☐ Yes	☐ No	$ _____
Have you closed/won any deals this week?	☐ Yes	☐ No	$ _____

Work it! a modern-day sales planner

NOTES

My Focus THIS WEEK

3 STEPS TO MAKING MY QUOTA

1. Identify: What are my focus accounts for this week?
These can include net new prospects, accounts on life support, prospects that have gone dark or a recent discovery meeting that you desperately need to turn into pipeline.

1. _____
2. _____
3. _____
4. _____
5. _____

2. Action: What are my action items this week?
This is not your to-do list. These are tasks that will create real movement and generate action in your accounts. Is it sending a follow-up email or scheduling a follow-up meeting? Is it making an executive connection or mapping out a mutual close plan?

_____
_____
_____
_____
_____
_____

PRO TIP #1: Spread these action items out over the next five days.
PRO TIP #2: These are action items you can take into your 1:1 with your manager.

3. Reflect: What results do I need to manifest this week?
These are things that need to happen this week to feel good about your efforts. Which dashboards or activity metrics do you need to hit? What housekeeping tasks have you been assigned by your manager or team?

_____
_____
_____
_____
_____
_____

My Prospecting THIS WEEK
WORKSHEET

The hardest part about prospecting is finding the time. So now, let's make time. Record your *Target Prospects* for this week. Then look at the different types of *Prospecting Activity* you can engage in and pick the activity (or activities) you are going to dedicate time to this week. This exercise is not meant to replace your bulk outreach. Rather, it's the time you will dedicate to understanding your accounts and their business priorities.

PRO TIP #1: Don't cheat. You can repeat target prospects in the same week. But NEVER repeat the same combination in the same week!

PRO TIP #2: These are great action items and strategies you can take into your 1:1 with your SDR/BDR for your weekly planning session.

Sunday	Monday	Tuesday	Wednesday	Thursday	Friday	Saturday

Target Prospects	
Account	1
Account	2
Account	3
Account	4
Account	5

Prospecting Activity	
Research *(web articles, executive interviews, press releases, annual report, etc.)*	A
Organizational mapping *(including any partners)*	B
Draft call or email scripts	C
Schedule call or email blitz	D
Other	E

NOTES

_____

_____

_____

_____

_____

| Su | M | Tu | W | Th | F | Sa |

DAILY INTENTION

Date _____

My quota this month is _____

The non-negotiables for myself:

☐ *Drink Water*
☐ *Move my body*
☐ *Be Awesome*

Target prospect:

To make notable movement in my accounts, today I will: - *List out activities from your weekly prospecting menu.* - *Act on the big things that will move the needle with your priority accounts.*	At this time:
☐	
☐	
☐	
☐	
☐	
☐	
☐	
☐	
☐	
☐	
☐	
☐	
☐	
☐	
☐	
☐	
☐	
☐	
☐	
☐	
☐	
☐	

Work it! a modern-day sales planner

NOTES

Su	M	Tu	W	Th	F	Sa

DAILY INTENTION

Date _____

My quota this month is _____

The non-negotiables for myself:

☐ *Drink Water*

☐ *Move my body*

☐ *Be Awesome*

Target prospect:

To make notable movement in my accounts, today I will: - *List out activities from your weekly prospecting menu.* - *Act on the big things that will move the needle with your priority accounts.*	At this time:
☐	
☐	
☐	
☐	
☐	
☐	
☐	
☐	
☐	
☐	
☐	
☐	
☐	
☐	
☐	
☐	
☐	
☐	
☐	
☐	
☐	
☐	

NOTES

| Su | M | Tu | W | Th | F | Sa |

DAILY INTENTION

Date _____

My quota this month is _____

The non-negotiables for myself:

☐ *Drink Water*
☐ *Move my body*
☐ *Be Awesome*

Target prospect: _____

To make notable movement in my accounts, today I will: - *List out activities from your weekly prospecting menu.* - *Act on the big things that will move the needle with your priority accounts.*	At this time:
☐	
☐	
☐	
☐	
☐	
☐	
☐	
☐	
☐	
☐	
☐	
☐	
☐	
☐	
☐	
☐	
☐	
☐	
☐	
☐	
☐	
☐	

NOTES

| Su | M | Tu | W | Th | F | Sa |

DAILY INTENTION

Date _____

My quota this month is _____

The non-negotiables for myself:

- ☐ *Drink Water*
- ☐ *Move my body*
- ☐ *Be Awesome*

Target prospect:

To make notable movement in my accounts, today I will: - *List out activities from your weekly prospecting menu.* - *Act on the big things that will move the needle with your priority accounts.*	At this time:
☐	
☐	
☐	
☐	
☐	
☐	
☐	
☐	
☐	
☐	
☐	
☐	
☐	
☐	
☐	
☐	
☐	
☐	
☐	
☐	
☐	
☐	

Work it! a modern-day sales planner

NOTES

Su | M | Tu | W | Th | F | Sa

DAILY INTENTION

Date _____

My quota this month is _____

The non-negotiables for myself:

□ *Drink Water*
□ *Move my body*
□ *Be Awesome*

Target prospect:

To make notable movement in my accounts, today I will: - *List out activities from your weekly prospecting menu.* - *Act on the big things that will move the needle with your priority accounts.*	At this time:
□	
□	
□	
□	
□	
□	
□	
□	
□	
□	
□	
□	
□	
□	
□	
□	
□	
□	
□	
□	
□	
□	

Work it! a modern-day sales planner

NOTES

Fri_YAY!

RECAP

+ **Your Peach**: What were you particularly proud of this week? Did you break into a new logo? Make a meaningful connection? Learn something new? Give a killer preso? Ink a deal? Write it down!

_____
_____
_____
_____

— **Your Pit**: Let's be real. Not everything goes as planned. What can you do better next week? Better time management? Did you skip a prospecting day? Not enought time to prepare for that important meeting? Write it down!

_____
_____
_____
_____

$ **Your Pipe**: Did you generate any new pipe this week? Are you close? What actions do you need to take to get your prospect or the awesome discovery call you had into your pipe? Before you forget, write it down as a starting point for your focus next week.

_____
_____
_____
_____

**Your Profile**: Let's look at the numbers.

Is your forecast up to date?	☐ Yes	☐ No	
Does your activity dashboard look good?	☐ Yes	☐ No	
Did you generate new pipeline this week?	☐ Yes	☐ No	$ _____
Have you closed/won any deals this week?	☐ Yes	☐ No	$ _____

Work it! a modern-day sales planner

NOTES

My Focus THIS WEEK
3 STEPS TO MAKING MY QUOTA

1. Identify: What are my focus accounts for this week?
These can include net new prospects, accounts on life support, prospects that have gone dark or a recent discovery meeting that you desperately need to turn into pipeline.

1. _____
2. _____
3. _____
4. _____
5. _____

2. Action: What are my action items this week?
This is not your to-do list. These are tasks that will create real movement and generate action in your accounts. Is it sending a follow-up email or scheduling a follow-up meeting? Is it making an executive connection or mapping out a mutual close plan?

_____
_____
_____
_____
_____
_____

PRO TIP #1: Spread these action items out over the next five days.
PRO TIP #2: These are action items you can take into your 1:1 with your manager.

3. Reflect: What results do I need to manifest this week?
These are things that need to happen this week to feel good about your efforts. Which dashboards or activity metrics do you need to hit? What housekeeping tasks have you been assigned by your manager or team?

_____
_____
_____
_____
_____
_____

Work it! a modern-day sales planner

My Prospecting THIS WEEK
WORKSHEET

The hardest part about prospecting is finding the time. So now, let's make time. Record your *Target Prospects* for this week. Then look at the different types of *Prospecting Activity* you can engage in and pick the activity (or activities) you are going to dedicate time to this week. This exercise is not meant to replace your bulk outreach. Rather, it's the time you will dedicate to understanding your accounts and their business priorities.

PRO TIP #1: Don't cheat. You can repeat target prospects in the same week. But NEVER repeat the same combination in the same week!

PRO TIP #2: These are great action items and strategies you can take into your 1:1 with your SDR/BDR for your weekly planning session.

Sunday	Monday	Tuesday	Wednesday	Thursday	Friday	Saturday

Target Prospects	
Account	1
Account	2
Account	3
Account	4
Account	5

Prospecting Activity	
Research (web articles, executive interviews, press releases, annual report, etc.)	A
Organizational mapping (including any partners)	B
Draft call or email scripts	C
Schedule call or email blitz	D
Other	E

NOTES

_____

_____

_____

_____

_____

Su	M	Tu	W	Th	F	Sa

DAILY INTENTION

Date _____

My quota this month is _____

The non-negotiables for myself:

- ☐ *Drink Water*
- ☐ *Move my body*
- ☐ *Be Awesome*

Target prospect:

To make notable movement in my accounts, today I will: - *List out activities from your weekly prospecting menu.* - *Act on the big things that will move the needle with your priority accounts.*	At this time:
☐	
☐	
☐	
☐	
☐	
☐	
☐	
☐	
☐	
☐	
☐	
☐	
☐	
☐	
☐	
☐	
☐	
☐	
☐	
☐	
☐	
☐	

NOTES

Su M Tu W Th F Sa

DAILY INTENTION

Date _____

My quota this month is _____

The non-negotiables for myself:

☐ *Drink Water*
☐ *Move my body*
☐ *Be Awesome*

Target prospect:

To make notable movement in my accounts, today I will: - *List out activities from your weekly prospecting menu.* - *Act on the big things that will move the needle with your priority accounts.*	At this time:
☐	
☐	
☐	
☐	
☐	
☐	
☐	
☐	
☐	
☐	
☐	
☐	
☐	
☐	
☐	
☐	
☐	
☐	
☐	
☐	
☐	
☐	

NOTES

DAILY INTENTION

Date _____

My quota this month is _____

The non-negotiables for myself:

- ☐ *Drink Water*
- ☐ *Move my body*
- ☐ *Be Awesome*

Target prospect:

To make notable movement in my accounts, today I will: - *List out activities from your weekly prospecting menu.* - *Act on the big things that will move the needle with your priority accounts.*	At this time:
☐	
☐	
☐	
☐	
☐	
☐	
☐	
☐	
☐	
☐	
☐	
☐	
☐	
☐	
☐	
☐	
☐	
☐	
☐	
☐	
☐	

NOTES

Su M Tu W Th F Sa

DAILY INTENTION

Date _____

My quota this month is _____

The non-negotiables for myself:

- ☐ *Drink Water*
- ☐ *Move my body*
- ☐ *Be Awesome*

Target prospect:

To make notable movement in my accounts, today I will: - *List out activities from your weekly prospecting menu.* - *Act on the big things that will move the needle with your priority accounts.*	At this time:
☐	
☐	
☐	
☐	
☐	
☐	
☐	
☐	
☐	
☐	
☐	
☐	
☐	
☐	
☐	
☐	
☐	
☐	
☐	
☐	
☐	
☐	

Work it! a modern-day sales planner

NOTES

| Su | M | Tu | W | Th | F | Sa |

DAILY INTENTION

Date _____

My quota this month is _____

The non-negotiables for myself:

- ☐ *Drink Water*
- ☐ *Move my body*
- ☐ *Be Awesome*

Target prospect:

To make notable movement in my accounts, today I will: - *List out activities from your weekly prospecting menu.* - *Act on the big things that will move the needle with your priority accounts.*	At this time:
☐	
☐	
☐	
☐	
☐	
☐	
☐	
☐	
☐	
☐	
☐	
☐	
☐	
☐	
☐	
☐	
☐	
☐	
☐	
☐	
☐	
☐	

NOTES

Fri _ YAY!

RECAP

+ **Your Peach**: What were you particularly proud of this week? Did you break into a new logo? Make a meaningful connection? Learn something new? Give a killer preso? Ink a deal? Write it down!

_____
_____
_____
_____

— **Your Pit**: Let's be real. Not everything goes as planned. What can you do better next week? Better time management? Did you skip a prospecting day? Not enought time to prepare for that important meeting? Write it down!

_____
_____
_____
_____

$ **Your Pipe**: Did you generate any new pipe this week? Are you close? What actions do you need to take to get your prospect or the awesome discovery call you had into your pipe? Before you forget, write it down as a starting point for your focus next week.

_____
_____
_____
_____

**Your Profile**: Let's look at the numbers.

Is your forecast up to date?	☐ Yes ☐ No	
Does your activity dashboard look good?	☐ Yes ☐ No	
Did you generate new pipeline this week?	☐ Yes ☐ No	$_____
Have you closed/won any deals this week?	☐ Yes ☐ No	$_____

NOTES

My Focus THIS WEEK
3 STEPS TO MAKING MY QUOTA

1. Identify: What are my focus accounts for this week?
These can include net new prospects, accounts on life support, prospects that have gone dark or a recent discovery meeting that you desperately need to turn into pipeline.

1. _____
2. _____
3. _____
4. _____
5. _____

2. Action: What are my action items this week?
This is not your to-do list. These are tasks that will create real movement and generate action in your accounts. Is it sending a follow-up email or scheduling a follow-up meeting? Is it making an executive connection or mapping out a mutual close plan?

_____
_____
_____
_____
_____
_____

PRO TIP #1: Spread these action items out over the next five days.
PRO TIP #2: These are action items you can take into your 1:1 with your manager.

3. Reflect: What results do I need to manifest this week?
These are things that need to happen this week to feel good about your efforts. Which dashboards or activity metrics do you need to hit? What housekeeping tasks have you been assigned by your manager or team?

_____
_____
_____
_____
_____
_____

Work it! a modern-day sales planner

My Prospecting THIS WEEK
WORKSHEET

The hardest part about prospecting is finding the time. So now, let's make time. Record your *Target Prospects* for this week. Then look at the different types of *Prospecting Activity* you can engage in and pick the activity (or activities) you are going to dedicate time to this week. This exercise is not meant to replace your bulk outreach. Rather, it's the time you will dedicate to understanding your accounts and their business priorities.

PRO TIP #1: Don't cheat. You can repeat target prospects in the same week. But NEVER repeat the same combination in the same week!

PRO TIP #2: These are great action items and strategies you can take into your 1:1 with your SDR/BDR for your weekly planning session.

Sunday	Monday	Tuesday	Wednesday	Thursday	Friday	Saturday

Target Prospects	
Account	1
Account	2
Account	3
Account	4
Account	5

Prospecting Activity	
Research *(web articles, executive interviews, press releases, annual report, etc.)*	A
Organizational mapping *(including any partners)*	B
Draft call or email scripts	C
Schedule call or email blitz	D
Other	E

NOTES

_____

_____

_____

_____

_____

Su M Tu W Th F Sa   *Date* _____

DAILY INTENTION

My quota this month is _____

The non-negotiables for myself:

- ☐ *Drink Water*
- ☐ *Move my body*
- ☐ *Be Awesome*

Target prospect:

To make notable movement in my accounts, today I will: - *List out activities from your weekly prospecting menu.* - *Act on the big things that will move the needle with your priority accounts.*	At this time:
☐	
☐	
☐	
☐	
☐	
☐	
☐	
☐	
☐	
☐	
☐	
☐	
☐	
☐	
☐	
☐	
☐	
☐	
☐	
☐	
☐	
☐	

NOTES

| Su | M | Tu | W | Th | F | Sa |

DAILY INTENTION

Date _____

My quota this month is _____

The non-negotiables for myself:

☐ *Drink Water*
☐ *Move my body*
☐ *Be Awesome*

Target prospect:

To make notable movement in my accounts, today I will: - *List out activities from your weekly prospecting menu.* - *Act on the big things that will move the needle with your priority accounts.*	At this time:
☐	
☐	
☐	
☐	
☐	
☐	
☐	
☐	
☐	
☐	
☐	
☐	
☐	
☐	
☐	
☐	
☐	
☐	
☐	
☐	
☐	
☐	

NOTES

Su | M | Tu | W | Th | F | Sa

DAILY INTENTION

Date _____

My quota this month is _____

The non-negotiables for myself:

- ☐ *Drink Water*
- ☐ *Move my body*
- ☐ *Be Awesome*

Target prospect:

To make notable movement in my accounts, today I will: - *List out activities from your weekly prospecting menu.* - *Act on the big things that will move the needle with your priority accounts.*	At this time:
☐	
☐	
☐	
☐	
☐	
☐	
☐	
☐	
☐	
☐	
☐	
☐	
☐	
☐	
☐	
☐	
☐	
☐	
☐	
☐	
☐	
☐	

NOTES

Su | M | Tu | W | Th | F | Sa

Date _____

DAILY INTENTION

My quota this month is _____

The non-negotiables for myself:

- ☐ *Drink Water*
- ☐ *Move my body*
- ☐ *Be Awesome*

Target prospect:

To make notable movement in my accounts, today I will: - *List out activities from your weekly prospecting menu.* - *Act on the big things that will move the needle with your priority accounts.*	At this time:
☐	
☐	
☐	
☐	
☐	
☐	
☐	
☐	
☐	
☐	
☐	
☐	
☐	
☐	
☐	
☐	
☐	
☐	
☐	
☐	
☐	
☐	

Work it! a modern-day sales planner

NOTES

Su | M | Tu | W | Th | F | Sa

DAILY INTENTION

Date _____

My quota this month is _____

The non-negotiables for myself:

☐ *Drink Water*

☐ *Move my body*

☐ *Be Awesome*

Target prospect:

To make notable movement in my accounts, today I will: - *List out activities from your weekly prospecting menu.* - *Act on the big things that will move the needle with your priority accounts.*	At this time:
☐	
☐	
☐	
☐	
☐	
☐	
☐	
☐	
☐	
☐	
☐	
☐	
☐	
☐	
☐	
☐	
☐	
☐	
☐	
☐	
☐	

NOTES

Fri_YAY!
RECAP

+ **Your Peach**: What were you particularly proud of this week? Did you break into a new logo? Make a meaningful connection? Learn something new? Give a killer preso? Ink a deal? Write it down!

_____

_____

_____

_____

– **Your Pit**: Let's be real. Not everything goes as planned. What can you do better next week? Better time management? Did you skip a prospecting day? Not enought time to prepare for that important meeting? Write it down!

_____

_____

_____

_____

$ **Your Pipe**: Did you generate any new pipe this week? Are you close? What actions do you need to take to get your prospect or the awesome discovery call you had into your pipe? Before you forget, write it down as a starting point for your focus next week.

_____

_____

_____

_____

**Your Profile**: Let's look at the numbers.

Is your forecast up to date?	☐ Yes	☐ No	
Does your activity dashboard look good?	☐ Yes	☐ No	
Did you generate new pipeline this week?	☐ Yes	☐ No	$ _____
Have you closed/won any deals this week?	☐ Yes	☐ No	$ _____

Work it! a modern-day sales planner

NOTES

My Quota Calculator

At the beginning of the month, take a moment to calculate and record your quota so it's top of mind.

My ANNUAL quota:

_____

My QUARTERLY quota:

q1 _____

q2 _____

q3 _____

q4 _____

My quota THIS MONTH:

_____

Are you on a ramp quota? Does your quota vary by month? Write it out.

CLOSED/WON to date:

_____

Notes

Sunday	Monday	Tuesday

My quota this month is

Wednesday	Thursday	Friday	Saturday

My Target Accounts

Write down your target account list here. It can be the entire list, your focus for the quarter, or your Tier 1 accounts. Simply write them down in a way that allows you to group them together for more efficient prospecting. Either way, use it as a quick reference to help you get organized so that you can get clarity on the accounts you want to focus on each day.

My Target Accounts

My Focus THIS WEEK
3 STEPS TO MAKING MY QUOTA

1. Identify: What are my focus accounts for this week?
These can include net new prospects, accounts on life support, prospects that have gone dark or a recent discovery meeting that you desperately need to turn into pipeline.

1. _____
2. _____
3. _____
4. _____
5. _____

2. Action: What are my action items this week?
This is not your to-do list. These are tasks that will create real movement and generate action in your accounts. Is it sending a follow-up email or scheduling a follow-up meeting? Is it making an executive connection or mapping out a mutual close plan?

_____
_____
_____
_____
_____
_____

PRO TIP #1: Spread these action items out over the next five days.
PRO TIP #2: These are action items you can take into your 1:1 with your manager.

3. Reflect: What results do I need to manifest this week?
These are things that need to happen this week to feel good about your efforts. Which dashboards or activity metrics do you need to hit? What housekeeping tasks have you been assigned by your manager or team?

_____
_____
_____
_____
_____
_____

Work it! a modern-day sales planner

My Prospecting THIS WEEK
WORKSHEET

The hardest part about prospecting is finding the time. So now, let's make time. Record your *Target Prospects* for this week. Then look at the different types of *Prospecting Activity* you can engage in and pick the activity (or activities) you are going to dedicate time to this week. This exercise is not meant to replace your bulk outreach. Rather, it's the time you will dedicate to understanding your accounts and their business priorities.

PRO TIP #1: Don't cheat. You can repeat target prospects in the same week. But NEVER repeat the same combination in the same week!

PRO TIP #2: These are great action items and strategies you can take into your 1:1 with your SDR/BDR for your weekly planning session.

Sunday	Monday	Tuesday	Wednesday	Thursday	Friday	Saturday

Target Prospects	
Account	1
Account	2
Account	3
Account	4
Account	5

Prospecting Activity	
Research *(web articles, executive interviews, press releases, annual report, etc.)*	A
Organizational mapping *(including any partners)*	B
Draft call or email scripts	C
Schedule call or email blitz	D
Other	E

NOTES

_____
_____
_____
_____
_____

Su	M	Tu	W	Th	F	Sa

DAILY INTENTION

Date _____

My quota this month is _____

The non-negotiables for myself:

- ☐ *Drink Water*
- ☐ *Move my body*
- ☐ *Be Awesome*

Target prospect:

To make notable movement in my accounts, today I will: - *List out activities from your weekly prospecting menu.* - *Act on the big things that will move the needle with your priority accounts.*	At this time:
☐	
☐	
☐	
☐	
☐	
☐	
☐	
☐	
☐	
☐	
☐	
☐	
☐	
☐	
☐	
☐	
☐	
☐	
☐	
☐	
☐	
☐	

Work it! a modern-day sales planner

NOTES

| Su | M | Tu | W | Th | F | Sa |

Date _____

DAILY INTENTION

My quota this month is _____

The non-negotiables for myself:

☐ *Drink Water*

☐ *Move my body*

☐ *Be Awesome*

Target prospect:

To make notable movement in my accounts, today I will: - *List out activities from your weekly prospecting menu.* - *Act on the big things that will move the needle with your priority accounts.*	At this time:
☐	
☐	
☐	
☐	
☐	
☐	
☐	
☐	
☐	
☐	
☐	
☐	
☐	
☐	
☐	
☐	
☐	
☐	
☐	
☐	
☐	

Work it! a modern-day sales planner

NOTES

Su | M | Tu | W | Th | F | Sa

DAILY INTENTION

Date _____

My quota this month is _____

The non-negotiables for myself:

☐ *Drink Water*

☐ *Move my body*

☐ *Be Awesome*

Target prospect:

To make notable movement in my accounts, today I will: - *List out activities from your weekly prospecting menu.* - *Act on the big things that will move the needle with your priority accounts.*	At this time:
☐	
☐	
☐	
☐	
☐	
☐	
☐	
☐	
☐	
☐	
☐	
☐	
☐	
☐	
☐	
☐	
☐	
☐	
☐	
☐	
☐	

Work it! a modern-day sales planner

NOTES

Su M Tu W Th F Sa   *Date* _____

DAILY INTENTION

My quota this month is _____

The non-negotiables for myself:

- ☐ *Drink Water*
- ☐ *Move my body*
- ☐ *Be Awesome*

Target prospect:

To make notable movement in my accounts, today I will: - *List out activities from your weekly prospecting menu.* - *Act on the big things that will move the needle with your priority accounts.*	At this time:
☐	
☐	
☐	
☐	
☐	
☐	
☐	
☐	
☐	
☐	
☐	
☐	
☐	
☐	
☐	
☐	
☐	
☐	
☐	
☐	
☐	
☐	

NOTES

| Su | M | Tu | W | Th | F | Sa |

DAILY INTENTION

Date _____

My quota this month is _____

The non-negotiables for myself:

☐ *Drink Water*

☐ *Move my body*

☐ *Be Awesome*

Target prospect:

To make notable movement in my accounts, today I will: - *List out activities from your weekly prospecting menu.* - *Act on the big things that will move the needle with your priority accounts.*	At this time:
☐	
☐	
☐	
☐	
☐	
☐	
☐	
☐	
☐	
☐	
☐	
☐	
☐	
☐	
☐	
☐	
☐	
☐	
☐	
☐	
☐	
☐	

Work it! a modern-day sales planner

NOTES

Fri_YAY!
RECAP

+ **Your Peach**: What were you particularly proud of this week? Did you break into a new logo? Make a meaningful connection? Learn something new? Give a killer preso? Ink a deal? Write it down!

_____
_____
_____
_____

— **Your Pit**: Let's be real. Not everything goes as planned. What can you do better next week? Better time management? Did you skip a prospecting day? Not enought time to prepare for that important meeting? Write it down!

_____
_____
_____
_____

$ **Your Pipe**: Did you generate any new pipe this week? Are you close? What actions do you need to take to get your prospect or the awesome discovery call you had into your pipe? Before you forget, write it down as a starting point for your focus next week.

_____
_____
_____
_____

**Your Profile**: Let's look at the numbers.

Is your forecast up to date?	☐ Yes	☐ No	
Does your activity dashboard look good?	☐ Yes	☐ No	
Did you generate new pipeline this week?	☐ Yes	☐ No	$ _____
Have you closed/won any deals this week?	☐ Yes	☐ No	$ _____

Work it! a modern-day sales planner

NOTES

My Focus THIS WEEK

3 STEPS TO MAKING MY QUOTA

1. Identify: What are my focus accounts for this week?
These can include net new prospects, accounts on life support, prospects that have gone dark or a recent discovery meeting that you desperately need to turn into pipeline.

1. _____
2. _____
3. _____
4. _____
5. _____

2. Action: What are my action items this week?
This is not your to-do list. These are tasks that will create real movement and generate action in your accounts. Is it sending a follow-up email or scheduling a follow-up meeting? Is it making an executive connection or mapping out a mutual close plan?

_____
_____
_____
_____
_____
_____

PRO TIP #1: Spread these action items out over the next five days.

PRO TIP #2: These are action items you can take into your 1:1 with your manager.

3. Reflect: What results do I need to manifest this week?
These are things that need to happen this week to feel good about your efforts. Which dashboards or activity metrics do you need to hit? What housekeeping tasks have you been assigned by your manager or team?

_____
_____
_____
_____
_____
_____

Work it! a modern-day sales planner

My Prospecting THIS WEEK
WORKSHEET

The hardest part about prospecting is finding the time. So now, let's make time. Record your *Target Prospects* for this week. Then look at the different types of *Prospecting Activity* you can engage in and pick the activity (or activities) you are going to dedicate time to this week. This exercise is not meant to replace your bulk outreach. Rather, it's the time you will dedicate to understanding your accounts and their business priorities.

PRO TIP #1: Don't cheat. You can repeat target prospects in the same week. But NEVER repeat the same combination in the same week!

PRO TIP #2: These are great action items and strategies you can take into your 1:1 with your SDR/BDR for your weekly planning session.

Sunday	Monday	Tuesday	Wednesday	Thursday	Friday	Saturday

Target Prospects	
Account	1
Account	2
Account	3
Account	4
Account	5

Prospecting Activity	
Research *(web articles, executive interviews, press releases, annual report, etc.)*	A
Organizational mapping *(including any partners)*	B
Draft call or email scripts	C
Schedule call or email blitz	D
Other	E

NOTES

_____

_____

_____

_____

_____

DAILY INTENTION

Date _____

My quota this month is _____

The non-negotiables for myself:

- ☐ *Drink Water*
- ☐ *Move my body*
- ☐ *Be Awesome*

Target prospect:

To make notable movement in my accounts, today I will: - *List out activities from your weekly prospecting menu.* - *Act on the big things that will move the needle with your priority accounts.*	At this time:
☐	
☐	
☐	
☐	
☐	
☐	
☐	
☐	
☐	
☐	
☐	
☐	
☐	
☐	
☐	
☐	
☐	
☐	
☐	
☐	
☐	
☐	

NOTES

| Su | M | Tu | W | Th | F | Sa |

DAILY INTENTION

Date _____

My quota this month is _____

The non-negotiables for myself:

- ☐ *Drink Water*
- ☐ *Move my body*
- ☐ *Be Awesome*

Target prospect:

To make notable movement in my accounts, today I will: - *List out activities from your weekly prospecting menu.* - *Act on the big things that will move the needle with your priority accounts.*	At this time:
☐	
☐	
☐	
☐	
☐	
☐	
☐	
☐	
☐	
☐	
☐	
☐	
☐	
☐	
☐	
☐	
☐	
☐	
☐	
☐	
☐	

Work it! a modern-day sales planner

NOTES

DAILY INTENTION

Date _____

My quota this month is _____

The non-negotiables for myself:

☐ *Drink Water*

☐ *Move my body*

☐ *Be Awesome*

Target prospect:

To make notable movement in my accounts, today I will: - *List out activities from your weekly prospecting menu.* - *Act on the big things that will move the needle with your priority accounts.*	At this time:
☐	
☐	
☐	
☐	
☐	
☐	
☐	
☐	
☐	
☐	
☐	
☐	
☐	
☐	
☐	
☐	
☐	
☐	
☐	
☐	
☐	

Work it! a modern-day sales planner

NOTES

DAILY INTENTION

Date _____

My quota this month is _____

The non-negotiables for myself:

- ☐ *Drink Water*
- ☐ *Move my body*
- ☐ *Be Awesome*

Target prospect:

To make notable movement in my accounts, today I will: - *List out activities from your weekly prospecting menu.* - *Act on the big things that will move the needle with your priority accounts.*	At this time:
☐	
☐	
☐	
☐	
☐	
☐	
☐	
☐	
☐	
☐	
☐	
☐	
☐	
☐	
☐	
☐	
☐	
☐	
☐	
☐	
☐	
☐	

NOTES

Su | M | Tu | W | Th | F | Sa

DAILY INTENTION

Date _____

My quota this month is _____

The non-negotiables for myself:

☐ *Drink Water*

☐ *Move my body*

☐ *Be Awesome*

Target prospect:

To make notable movement in my accounts, today I will: - *List out activities from your weekly prospecting menu.* - *Act on the big things that will move the needle with your priority accounts.*	At this time:
☐	
☐	
☐	
☐	
☐	
☐	
☐	
☐	
☐	
☐	
☐	
☐	
☐	
☐	
☐	
☐	
☐	
☐	
☐	
☐	
☐	
☐	

Work it! a modern-day sales planner

NOTES

Fri _ YAY!

RECAP

+ **Your Peach**: What were you particularly proud of this week? Did you break into a new logo? Make a meaningful connection? Learn something new? Give a killer preso? Ink a deal? Write it down!

_____

_____

_____

_____

— **Your Pit**: Let's be real. Not everything goes as planned. What can you do better next week? Better time management? Did you skip a prospecting day? Not enought time to prepare for that important meeting? Write it down!

_____

_____

_____

_____

$ **Your Pipe**: Did you generate any new pipe this week? Are you close? What actions do you need to take to get your prospect or the awesome discovery call you had into your pipe? Before you forget, write it down as a starting point for your focus next week.

_____

_____

_____

_____

**Your Profile**: Let's look at the numbers.

Is your forecast up to date?	☐ Yes	☐ No	
Does your activity dashboard look good?	☐ Yes	☐ No	
Did you generate new pipeline this week?	☐ Yes	☐ No	$ _____
Have you closed/won any deals this week?	☐ Yes	☐ No	$ _____

Work it! a modern-day sales planner

NOTES

My Focus THIS WEEK
3 STEPS TO MAKING MY QUOTA

1. Identify: What are my focus accounts for this week?
These can include net new prospects, accounts on life support, prospects that have gone dark or a recent discovery meeting that you desperately need to turn into pipeline.

1. _____
2. _____
3. _____
4. _____
5. _____

2. Action: What are my action items this week?
This is not your to-do list. These are tasks that will create real movement and generate action in your accounts. Is it sending a follow-up email or scheduling a follow-up meeting? Is it making an executive connection or mapping out a mutual close plan?

_____
_____
_____
_____
_____
_____

PRO TIP #1: Spread these action items out over the next five days.
PRO TIP #2: These are action items you can take into your 1:1 with your manager.

3. Reflect: What results do I need to manifest this week?
These are things that need to happen this week to feel good about your efforts. Which dashboards or activity metrics do you need to hit? What housekeeping tasks have you been assigned by your manager or team?

_____
_____
_____
_____
_____
_____

Work it! a modern-day sales planner

My Prospecting THIS WEEK
WORKSHEET

The hardest part about prospecting is finding the time. So now, let's make time. Record your *Target Prospects* for this week. Then look at the different types of *Prospecting Activity* you can engage in and pick the activity (or activities) you are going to dedicate time to this week. This exercise is not meant to replace your bulk outreach. Rather, it's the time you will dedicate to understanding your accounts and their business priorities.

PRO TIP #1: Don't cheat. You can repeat target prospects in the same week. But NEVER repeat the same combination in the same week!

PRO TIP #2: These are great action items and strategies you can take into your 1:1 with your SDR/BDR for your weekly planning session.

Sunday	Monday	Tuesday	Wednesday	Thursday	Friday	Saturday

Target Prospects	
Account	1
Account	2
Account	3
Account	4
Account	5

Prospecting Activity	
Research (web articles, executive interviews, press releases, annual report, etc.)	A
Organizational mapping (including any partners)	B
Draft call or email scripts	C
Schedule call or email blitz	D
Other	E

NOTES

_____

_____

_____

_____

_____

Su M Tu W Th F Sa   *Date* _____

DAILY INTENTION   *My quota this month is* _____

The non-negotiables for myself: Target prospect:

□ *Drink Water*
□ *Move my body*
□ *Be Awesome*

To make notable movement in my accounts, today I will: - *List out activities from your weekly prospecting menu.* - *Act on the big things that will move the needle with your priority accounts.*	At this time:
□	
□	
□	
□	
□	
□	
□	
□	
□	
□	
□	
□	
□	
□	
□	
□	
□	
□	
□	
□	
□	
□	

Work it! a modern-day sales planner

NOTES

Su | M | Tu | W | Th | F | Sa

DAILY INTENTION

Date _____

My quota this month is _____

The non-negotiables for myself:

- ☐ *Drink Water*
- ☐ *Move my body*
- ☐ *Be Awesome*

Target prospect:

To make notable movement in my accounts, today I will: - *List out activities from your weekly prospecting menu.* - *Act on the big things that will move the needle with your priority accounts.*	At this time:
☐	
☐	
☐	
☐	
☐	
☐	
☐	
☐	
☐	
☐	
☐	
☐	
☐	
☐	
☐	
☐	
☐	
☐	
☐	
☐	
☐	
☐	

NOTES

| Su | M | Tu | W | Th | F | Sa |

Date _____

DAILY INTENTION

My quota this month is _____

The non-negotiables for myself:

- ☐ *Drink Water*
- ☐ *Move my body*
- ☐ *Be Awesome*

Target prospect:

To make notable movement in my accounts, today I will: - *List out activities from your weekly prospecting menu.* - *Act on the big things that will move the needle with your priority accounts.*	At this time:
☐	
☐	
☐	
☐	
☐	
☐	
☐	
☐	
☐	
☐	
☐	
☐	
☐	
☐	
☐	
☐	
☐	
☐	
☐	
☐	
☐	
☐	

Work it! a modern-day sales planner

NOTES

DAILY INTENTION

Date _____

My quota this month is _____

The non-negotiables for myself:

- ☐ *Drink Water*
- ☐ *Move my body*
- ☐ *Be Awesome*

Target prospect:

To make notable movement in my accounts, today I will: - *List out activities from your weekly prospecting menu.* - *Act on the big things that will move the needle with your priority accounts.*	At this time:
☐	
☐	
☐	
☐	
☐	
☐	
☐	
☐	
☐	
☐	
☐	
☐	
☐	
☐	
☐	
☐	
☐	
☐	
☐	
☐	
☐	
☐	

Work it! a modern-day sales planner

NOTES

Su M Tu W Th F Sa   *Date* _____

DAILY INTENTION

My quota this month is _____

The non-negotiables for myself:

- ☐ *Drink Water*
- ☐ *Move my body*
- ☐ *Be Awesome*

Target prospect:

To make notable movement in my accounts, today I will: - *List out activities from your weekly prospecting menu.* - *Act on the big things that will move the needle with your priority accounts.*	At this time:
☐	
☐	
☐	
☐	
☐	
☐	
☐	
☐	
☐	
☐	
☐	
☐	
☐	
☐	
☐	
☐	
☐	
☐	
☐	
☐	
☐	
☐	

Work it! a modern-day sales planner

NOTES

Fri_YAY!

RECAP

+ **Your Peach**: What were you particularly proud of this week? Did you break into a new logo? Make a meaningful connection? Learn something new? Give a killer preso? Ink a deal? Write it down!

_____

_____

_____

_____

− **Your Pit**: Let's be real. Not everything goes as planned. What can you do better next week? Better time management? Did you skip a prospecting day? Not enought time to prepare for that important meeting? Write it down!

_____

_____

_____

_____

$ **Your Pipe**: Did you generate any new pipe this week? Are you close? What actions do you need to take to get your prospect or the awesome discovery call you had into your pipe? Before you forget, write it down as a starting point for your focus next week.

_____

_____

_____

_____

**Your Profile**: Let's look at the numbers.

Is your forecast up to date?	☐ Yes ☐ No	
Does your activity dashboard look good?	☐ Yes ☐ No	
Did you generate new pipeline this week?	☐ Yes ☐ No	$ _____
Have you closed/won any deals this week?	☐ Yes ☐ No	$ _____

Work it! a modern-day sales planner

NOTES

My Focus THIS WEEK
3 STEPS TO MAKING MY QUOTA

1. Identify: What are my focus accounts for this week?
These can include net new prospects, accounts on life support, prospects that have gone dark or a recent discovery meeting that you desperately need to turn into pipeline.

1. _____
2. _____
3. _____
4. _____
5. _____

2. Action: What are my action items this week?
This is not your to-do list. These are tasks that will create real movement and generate action in your accounts. Is it sending a follow-up email or scheduling a follow-up meeting? Is it making an executive connection or mapping out a mutual close plan?

_____
_____
_____
_____
_____
_____

PRO TIP #1: Spread these action items out over the next five days.

PRO TIP #2: These are action items you can take into your 1:1 with your manager.

3. Reflect: What results do I need to manifest this week?
These are things that need to happen this week to feel good about your efforts. Which dashboards or activity metrics do you need to hit? What housekeeping tasks have you been assigned by your manager or team?

_____
_____
_____
_____
_____
_____

Work it! a modern-day sales planner

My Prospecting THIS WEEK
WORKSHEET

The hardest part about prospecting is finding the time. So now, let's make time. Record your *Target Prospects* for this week. Then look at the different types of *Prospecting Activity* you can engage in and pick the activity (or activities) you are going to dedicate time to this week. This exercise is not meant to replace your bulk outreach. Rather, it's the time you will dedicate to understanding your accounts and their business priorities.

PRO TIP #1: Don't cheat. You can repeat target prospects in the same week. But NEVER repeat the same combination in the same week!

PRO TIP #2: These are great action items and strategies you can take into your 1:1 with your SDR/BDR for your weekly planning session.

Sunday	Monday	Tuesday	Wednesday	Thursday	Friday	Saturday

Target Prospects	
Account	1
Account	2
Account	3
Account	4
Account	5

Prospecting Activity	
Research *(web articles, executive interviews, press releases, annual report, etc.)*	A
Organizational mapping *(including any partners)*	B
Draft call or email scripts	C
Schedule call or email blitz	D
Other	E

NOTES

_____

_____

_____

_____

_____

Su M Tu W Th F Sa   Date _____

DAILY INTENTION   *My quota this month is* _____

The non-negotiables for myself: Target prospect:

☐ *Drink Water*

☐ *Move my body*

☐ *Be Awesome*

To make notable movement in my accounts, today I will: - *List out activities from your weekly prospecting menu.* - *Act on the big things that will move the needle with your priority accounts.*	At this time:
☐	
☐	
☐	
☐	
☐	
☐	
☐	
☐	
☐	
☐	
☐	
☐	
☐	
☐	
☐	
☐	
☐	
☐	
☐	
☐	
☐	
☐	

Work it! a modern-day sales planner

NOTES

Su	M	Tu	W	Th	F	Sa

DAILY INTENTION

Date _____

My quota this month is _____

The non-negotiables for myself:

- ☐ *Drink Water*
- ☐ *Move my body*
- ☐ *Be Awesome*

Target prospect:

To make notable movement in my accounts, today I will: - *List out activities from your weekly prospecting menu.* - *Act on the big things that will move the needle with your priority accounts.*	At this time:
☐	
☐	
☐	
☐	
☐	
☐	
☐	
☐	
☐	
☐	
☐	
☐	
☐	
☐	
☐	
☐	
☐	
☐	
☐	
☐	
☐	
☐	

Work it! a modern-day sales planner

NOTES

DAILY INTENTION

Date _____

My quota this month is _____

The non-negotiables for myself:

☐ *Drink Water*

☐ *Move my body*

☐ *Be Awesome*

Target prospect:

To make notable movement in my accounts, today I will: - *List out activities from your weekly prospecting menu.* - *Act on the big things that will move the needle with your priority accounts.*	At this time:
☐	
☐	
☐	
☐	
☐	
☐	
☐	
☐	
☐	
☐	
☐	
☐	
☐	
☐	
☐	
☐	
☐	
☐	
☐	
☐	
☐	
☐	

NOTES

DAILY INTENTION

My quota this month is _____

The non-negotiables for myself:

☐ *Drink Water*
☐ *Move my body*
☐ *Be Awesome*

Target prospect:

To make notable movement in my accounts, today I will: - *List out activities from your weekly prospecting menu.* - *Act on the big things that will move the needle with your priority accounts.*	At this time:
☐	
☐	
☐	
☐	
☐	
☐	
☐	
☐	
☐	
☐	
☐	
☐	
☐	
☐	
☐	
☐	
☐	
☐	
☐	
☐	
☐	
☐	

NOTES

| Su | M | Tu | W | Th | F | Sa |

DAILY INTENTION

Date _____

My quota this month is _____

The non-negotiables for myself:

☐ *Drink Water*
☐ *Move my body*
☐ *Be Awesome*

Target prospect:

To make notable movement in my accounts, today I will: - *List out activities from your weekly prospecting menu.* - *Act on the big things that will move the needle with your priority accounts.*	At this time:
☐	
☐	
☐	
☐	
☐	
☐	
☐	
☐	
☐	
☐	
☐	
☐	
☐	
☐	
☐	
☐	
☐	
☐	
☐	
☐	
☐	
☐	

Work it! a modern-day sales planner

NOTES

Fri _ YAY!

RECAP

+ **Your Peach**: What were you particularly proud of this week? Did you break into a new logo? Make a meaningful connection? Learn something new? Give a killer preso? Ink a deal? Write it down!

_____

_____

_____

_____

— **Your Pit**: Let's be real. Not everything goes as planned. What can you do better next week? Better time management? Did you skip a prospecting day? Not enought time to prepare for that important meeting? Write it down!

_____

_____

_____

_____

$ **Your Pipe**: Did you generate any new pipe this week? Are you close? What actions do you need to take to get your prospect or the awesome discovery call you had into your pipe? Before you forget, write it down as a starting point for your focus next week.

_____

_____

_____

_____

**Your Profile**: Let's look at the numbers.

Is your forecast up to date?	☐ Yes	☐ No
Does your activity dashboard look good?	☐ Yes	☐ No
Did you generate new pipeline this week?	☐ Yes	☐ No $ _____
Have you closed/won any deals this week?	☐ Yes	☐ No $ _____

Work it! a modern-day sales planner

NOTES

My Quota Calculator
At the beginning of the month, take a moment to calculate and record your quota so it's top of mind.

My ANNUAL quota:

_____

My QUARTERLY quota:

q1 _____

q2 _____

q3 _____

q4 _____

My quota THIS MONTH:

_____

Are you on a ramp quota? Does your quota vary by month? Write it out.

CLOSED/WON to date:

_____

Notes

Sunday	Monday	Tuesday

My quota this month is

Wednesday	Thursday	Friday	Saturday

My Target Accounts

Write down your target account list here. It can be the entire list, your focus for the quarter, or your Tier 1 accounts. Simply write them down in a way that allows you to group them together for more efficient prospecting. Either way, use it as a quick reference to help you get organized so that you can get clarity on the accounts you want to focus on each day.

My Target Accounts

My Focus THIS WEEK
3 STEPS TO MAKING MY QUOTA

1. Identify: What are my focus accounts for this week?
These can include net new prospects, accounts on life support, prospects that have gone dark or a recent discovery meeting that you desperately need to turn into pipeline.

1. _____
2. _____
3. _____
4. _____
5. _____

2. Action: What are my action items this week?
This is not your to-do list. These are tasks that will create real movement and generate action in your accounts. Is it sending a follow-up email or scheduling a follow-up meeting? Is it making an executive connection or mapping out a mutual close plan?

_____
_____
_____
_____
_____
_____

PRO TIP #1: Spread these action items out over the next five days.
PRO TIP #2: These are action items you can take into your 1:1 with your manager.

3. Reflect: What results do I need to manifest this week?
These are things that need to happen this week to feel good about your efforts. Which dashboards or activity metrics do you need to hit? What housekeeping tasks have you been assigned by your manager or team?

_____
_____
_____
_____
_____
_____

Work it! a modern-day sales planner

My Prospecting THIS WEEK
WORKSHEET

The hardest part about prospecting is finding the time. So now, let's make time. Record your *Target Prospects* for this week. Then look at the different types of *Prospecting Activity* you can engage in and pick the activity (or activities) you are going to dedicate time to this week. This exercise is not meant to replace your bulk outreach. Rather, it's the time you will dedicate to understanding your accounts and their business priorities.

PRO TIP #1: Don't cheat. You can repeat target prospects in the same week. But NEVER repeat the same combination in the same week!

PRO TIP #2: These are great action items and strategies you can take into your 1:1 with your SDR/BDR for your weekly planning session.

Sunday	Monday	Tuesday	Wednesday	Thursday	Friday	Saturday

Target Prospects	
Account	1
Account	2
Account	3
Account	4
Account	5

Prospecting Activity	
Research (web articles, executive interviews, press releases, annual report, etc.)	A
Organizational mapping (including any partners)	B
Draft call or email scripts	C
Schedule call or email blitz	D
Other	E

NOTES

_____

_____

_____

_____

_____

Su | M | Tu | W | Th | F | Sa

DAILY INTENTION

Date _____

My quota this month is _____

The non-negotiables for myself:

- ☐ *Drink Water*
- ☐ *Move my body*
- ☐ *Be Awesome*

Target prospect:

To make notable movement in my accounts, today I will: - *List out activities from your weekly prospecting menu.* - *Act on the big things that will move the needle with your priority accounts.*	At this time:
☐	
☐	
☐	
☐	
☐	
☐	
☐	
☐	
☐	
☐	
☐	
☐	
☐	
☐	
☐	
☐	
☐	
☐	
☐	
☐	
☐	
☐	

NOTES

Su | M | Tu | W | Th | F | Sa   *Date* _____

DAILY INTENTION

My quota this month is _____

The non-negotiables for myself:

☐ *Drink Water*
☐ *Move my body*
☐ *Be Awesome*

Target prospect:

To make notable movement in my accounts, today I will: - *List out activities from your weekly prospecting menu.* - *Act on the big things that will move the needle with your priority accounts.*	At this time:
☐	
☐	
☐	
☐	
☐	
☐	
☐	
☐	
☐	
☐	
☐	
☐	
☐	
☐	
☐	
☐	
☐	
☐	
☐	
☐	
☐	
☐	

Work it! a modern-day sales planner

NOTES

Su M Tu W Th F Sa   Date _____

DAILY INTENTION

My quota this month is _____

The non-negotiables for myself:

□ *Drink Water*
□ *Move my body*
□ *Be Awesome*

Target prospect:

To make notable movement in my accounts, today I will: - *List out activities from your weekly prospecting menu.* - *Act on the big things that will move the needle with your priority accounts.*	At this time:
□	
□	
□	
□	
□	
□	
□	
□	
□	
□	
□	
□	
□	
□	
□	
□	
□	
□	
□	
□	
□	
□	

NOTES

Su | M | Tu | W | Th | F | Sa

DAILY INTENTION

Date _____

My quota this month is _____

The non-negotiables for myself:

☐ *Drink Water*
☐ *Move my body*
☐ *Be Awesome*

Target prospect:

To make notable movement in my accounts, today I will: - *List out activities from your weekly prospecting menu.* - *Act on the big things that will move the needle with your priority accounts.*	At this time:
☐	
☐	
☐	
☐	
☐	
☐	
☐	
☐	
☐	
☐	
☐	
☐	
☐	
☐	
☐	
☐	
☐	
☐	
☐	
☐	
☐	
☐	

Work it! a modern-day sales planner

NOTES

Su	M	Tu	W	Th	F	Sa

DAILY INTENTION

Date _____

My quota this month is _____

The non-negotiables for myself:

- ☐ *Drink Water*
- ☐ *Move my body*
- ☐ *Be Awesome*

Target prospect:

To make notable movement in my accounts, today I will: - *List out activities from your weekly prospecting menu.* - *Act on the big things that will move the needle with your priority accounts.*	At this time:
☐	
☐	
☐	
☐	
☐	
☐	
☐	
☐	
☐	
☐	
☐	
☐	
☐	
☐	
☐	
☐	
☐	
☐	
☐	
☐	
☐	
☐	

NOTES

Fri_YAY!
RECAP

+ **Your Peach**: What were you particularly proud of this week? Did you break into a new logo? Make a meaningful connection? Learn something new? Give a killer preso? Ink a deal? Write it down!

_____

_____

_____

_____

— **Your Pit**: Let's be real. Not everything goes as planned. What can you do better next week? Better time management? Did you skip a prospecting day? Not enought time to prepare for that important meeting? Write it down!

_____

_____

_____

_____

$ **Your Pipe**: Did you generate any new pipe this week? Are you close? What actions do you need to take to get your prospect or the awesome discovery call you had into your pipe? Before you forget, write it down as a starting point for your focus next week.

_____

_____

_____

_____

**Your Profile**: Let's look at the numbers.

Is your forecast up to date?	☐ Yes	☐ No	
Does your activity dashboard look good?	☐ Yes	☐ No	
Did you generate new pipeline this week?	☐ Yes	☐ No	$ _____
Have you closed/won any deals this week?	☐ Yes	☐ No	$ _____

Work it! a modern-day sales planner

NOTES

My Focus THIS WEEK
3 STEPS TO MAKING MY QUOTA

1. Identify: What are my focus accounts for this week?
These can include net new prospects, accounts on life support, prospects that have gone dark or a recent discovery meeting that you desperately need to turn into pipeline.

1. _____
2. _____
3. _____
4. _____
5. _____

2. Action: What are my action items this week?
This is not your to-do list. These are tasks that will create real movement and generate action in your accounts. Is it sending a follow-up email or scheduling a follow-up meeting? Is it making an executive connection or mapping out a mutual close plan?

_____
_____
_____
_____
_____
_____

PRO TIP #1: Spread these action items out over the next five days.
PRO TIP #2: These are action items you can take into your 1:1 with your manager.

3. Reflect: What results do I need to manifest this week?
These are things that need to happen this week to feel good about your efforts. Which dashboards or activity metrics do you need to hit? What housekeeping tasks have you been assigned by your manager or team?

_____
_____
_____
_____
_____
_____

Work it! a modern-day sales planner

My Prospecting THIS WEEK

WORKSHEET

The hardest part about prospecting is finding the time. So now, let's make time. Record your *Target Prospects* for this week. Then look at the different types of *Prospecting Activity* you can engage in and pick the activity (or activities) you are going to dedicate time to this week. This exercise is not meant to replace your bulk outreach. Rather, it's the time you will dedicate to understanding your accounts and their business priorities.

PRO TIP #1: Don't cheat. You can repeat target prospects in the same week. But NEVER repeat the same combination in the same week!

PRO TIP #2: These are great action items and strategies you can take into your 1:1 with your SDR/BDR for your weekly planning session.

Sunday	Monday	Tuesday	Wednesday	Thursday	Friday	Saturday

Target Prospects	
Account	1
Account	2
Account	3
Account	4
Account	5

Prospecting Activity	
Research *(web articles, executive interviews, press releases, annual report, etc.)*	A
Organizational mapping *(including any partners)*	B
Draft call or email scripts	C
Schedule call or email blitz	D
Other	E

NOTES

_____

_____

_____

_____

_____

| Su | M | Tu | W | Th | F | Sa |

DAILY INTENTION

Date _____

My quota this month is _____

The non-negotiables for myself:

☐ *Drink Water*

☐ *Move my body*

☐ *Be Awesome*

Target prospect:

To make notable movement in my accounts, today I will: - *List out activities from your weekly prospecting menu.* - *Act on the big things that will move the needle with your priority accounts.*	At this time:
☐	
☐	
☐	
☐	
☐	
☐	
☐	
☐	
☐	
☐	
☐	
☐	
☐	
☐	
☐	
☐	
☐	
☐	
☐	
☐	
☐	
☐	

Work it! a modern-day sales planner

NOTES

Su M Tu W Th F Sa   *Date* _____

DAILY INTENTION

My quota this month is _____

The non-negotiables for myself:

- ☐ *Drink Water*
- ☐ *Move my body*
- ☐ *Be Awesome*

Target prospect:

To make notable movement in my accounts, today I will: *- List out activities from your weekly prospecting menu.* *- Act on the big things that will move the needle with your priority accounts.*	At this time:
☐	
☐	
☐	
☐	
☐	
☐	
☐	
☐	
☐	
☐	
☐	
☐	
☐	
☐	
☐	
☐	
☐	
☐	
☐	
☐	
☐	
☐	

Work it! a modern-day sales planner

NOTES

Su M Tu W Th F Sa Date _____

DAILY INTENTION

My quota this month is _____

The non-negotiables for myself:

☐ *Drink Water*

☐ *Move my body*

☐ *Be Awesome*

Target prospect:

To make notable movement in my accounts, today I will: - *List out activities from your weekly prospecting menu.* - *Act on the big things that will move the needle with your priority accounts.*	At this time:
☐	
☐	
☐	
☐	
☐	
☐	
☐	
☐	
☐	
☐	
☐	
☐	
☐	
☐	
☐	
☐	
☐	
☐	
☐	
☐	
☐	
☐	

Work it! a modern-day sales planner

NOTES

DAILY INTENTION

Date _____

My quota this month is _____

The non-negotiables for myself:

- ☐ *Drink Water*
- ☐ *Move my body*
- ☐ *Be Awesome*

Target prospect:

To make notable movement in my accounts, today I will: - *List out activities from your weekly prospecting menu.* - *Act on the big things that will move the needle with your priority accounts.*	At this time:
☐	
☐	
☐	
☐	
☐	
☐	
☐	
☐	
☐	
☐	
☐	
☐	
☐	
☐	
☐	
☐	
☐	
☐	
☐	
☐	
☐	
☐	

Work it! a modern-day sales planner

NOTES

Su M Tu W Th F Sa

DAILY INTENTION

Date _____

My quota this month is _____

The non-negotiables for myself:

☐ *Drink Water*

☐ *Move my body*

☐ *Be Awesome*

Target prospect:

To make notable movement in my accounts, today I will: - *List out activities from your weekly prospecting menu.* - *Act on the big things that will move the needle with your priority accounts.*	At this time:
☐	
☐	
☐	
☐	
☐	
☐	
☐	
☐	
☐	
☐	
☐	
☐	
☐	
☐	
☐	
☐	
☐	
☐	
☐	
☐	
☐	
☐	

NOTES

Fri_YAY!

RECAP

+ **Your Peach**: What were you particularly proud of this week? Did you break into a new logo? Make a meaningful connection? Learn something new? Give a killer preso? Ink a deal? Write it down!

_____

_____

_____

_____

— **Your Pit**: Let's be real. Not everything goes as planned. What can you do better next week? Better time management? Did you skip a prospecting day? Not enought time to prepare for that important meeting? Write it down!

_____

_____

_____

_____

$ **Your Pipe**: Did you generate any new pipe this week? Are you close? What actions do you need to take to get your prospect or the awesome discovery call you had into your pipe? Before you forget, write it down as a starting point for your focus next week.

_____

_____

_____

_____

**Your Profile**: Let's look at the numbers.

Is your forecast up to date?	☐ Yes	☐ No	
Does your activity dashboard look good?	☐ Yes	☐ No	
Did you generate new pipeline this week?	☐ Yes	☐ No	$_____
Have you closed/won any deals this week?	☐ Yes	☐ No	$_____

Work it! a modern-day sales planner

NOTES

My Focus THIS WEEK

3 STEPS TO MAKING MY QUOTA

1. Identify: What are my focus accounts for this week?

These can include net new prospects, accounts on life support, prospects that have gone dark or a recent discovery meeting that you desperately need to turn into pipeline.

1. _____
2. _____
3. _____
4. _____
5. _____

2. Action: What are my action items this week?

This is not your to-do list. These are tasks that will create real movement and generate action in your accounts. Is it sending a follow-up email or scheduling a follow-up meeting? Is it making an executive connection or mapping out a mutual close plan?

_____
_____
_____
_____
_____
_____

PRO TIP #1: Spread these action items out over the next five days.

PRO TIP #2: These are action items you can take into your 1:1 with your manager.

3. Reflect: What results do I need to manifest this week?

These are things that need to happen this week to feel good about your efforts. Which dashboards or activity metrics do you need to hit? What housekeeping tasks have you been assigned by your manager or team?

_____
_____
_____
_____
_____
_____

Work it! a modern-day sales planner

My Prospecting THIS WEEK
WORKSHEET

The hardest part about prospecting is finding the time. So now, let's make time. Record your *Target Prospects* for this week. Then look at the different types of *Prospecting Activity* you can engage in and pick the activity (or activities) you are going to dedicate time to this week. This exercise is not meant to replace your bulk outreach. Rather, it's the time you will dedicate to understanding your accounts and their business priorities.

PRO TIP #1: Don't cheat. You can repeat target prospects in the same week. But NEVER repeat the same combination in the same week!

PRO TIP #2: These are great action items and strategies you can take into your 1:1 with your SDR/BDR for your weekly planning session.

Sunday	Monday	Tuesday	Wednesday	Thursday	Friday	Saturday

Target Prospects	
Account	1
Account	2
Account	3
Account	4
Account	5

Prospecting Activity	
Research *(web articles, executive interviews, press releases, annual report, etc.)*	A
Organizational mapping *(including any partners)*	B
Draft call or email scripts	C
Schedule call or email blitz	D
Other	E

NOTES

_____

_____

_____

_____

_____

Su | M | Tu | W | Th | F | Sa

DAILY INTENTION

Date _____

My quota this month is _____

The non-negotiables for myself:

☐ *Drink Water*
☐ *Move my body*
☐ *Be Awesome*

Target prospect:

To make notable movement in my accounts, today I will: - *List out activities from your weekly prospecting menu.* - *Act on the big things that will move the needle with your priority accounts.*	At this time:
☐	
☐	
☐	
☐	
☐	
☐	
☐	
☐	
☐	
☐	
☐	
☐	
☐	
☐	
☐	
☐	
☐	
☐	
☐	
☐	
☐	
☐	

Work it! a modern-day sales planner

NOTES

Su | M | Tu | W | Th | F | Sa

DAILY INTENTION

Date _____

My quota this month is _____

The non-negotiables for myself:

☐ *Drink Water*
☐ *Move my body*
☐ *Be Awesome*

Target prospect:

To make notable movement in my accounts, today I will: - *List out activities from your weekly prospecting menu.* - *Act on the big things that will move the needle with your priority accounts.*	At this time:
☐	
☐	
☐	
☐	
☐	
☐	
☐	
☐	
☐	
☐	
☐	
☐	
☐	
☐	
☐	
☐	
☐	
☐	
☐	
☐	
☐	
☐	

Work it! a modern-day sales planner

NOTES

Su | M | Tu | W | Th | F | Sa

DAILY INTENTION

Date _____

My quota this month is _____

The non-negotiables for myself:

☐ *Drink Water*
☐ *Move my body*
☐ *Be Awesome*

Target prospect:

To make notable movement in my accounts, today I will: - *List out activities from your weekly prospecting menu.* - *Act on the big things that will move the needle with your priority accounts.*	At this time:
☐	
☐	
☐	
☐	
☐	
☐	
☐	
☐	
☐	
☐	
☐	
☐	
☐	
☐	
☐	
☐	
☐	
☐	
☐	
☐	
☐	

Work it! a modern-day sales planner

NOTES

DAILY INTENTION

Date _____

My quota this month is _____

The non-negotiables for myself:

☐ Drink Water
☐ Move my body
☐ Be Awesome

Target prospect:

To make notable movement in my accounts, today I will: - *List out activities from your weekly prospecting menu.* - *Act on the big things that will move the needle with your priority accounts.*	At this time:
☐	
☐	
☐	
☐	
☐	
☐	
☐	
☐	
☐	
☐	
☐	
☐	
☐	
☐	
☐	
☐	
☐	
☐	
☐	
☐	
☐	
☐	

Work it! a modern-day sales planner

NOTES

DAILY INTENTION

My quota this month is _____

The non-negotiables for myself:

☐ *Drink Water*

☐ *Move my body*

☐ *Be Awesome*

Target prospect:

To make notable movement in my accounts, today I will: - *List out activities from your weekly prospecting menu.* - *Act on the big things that will move the needle with your priority accounts.*	At this time:
☐	
☐	
☐	
☐	
☐	
☐	
☐	
☐	
☐	
☐	
☐	
☐	
☐	
☐	
☐	
☐	
☐	
☐	
☐	
☐	
☐	
☐	

NOTES

Fri _ YAY!
RECAP

+

Your Peach: What were you particularly proud of this week? Did you break into a new logo? Make a meaningful connection? Learn something new? Give a killer preso? Ink a deal? Write it down!

_____

_____

_____

_____

—

Your Pit: Let's be real. Not everything goes as planned. What can you do better next week? Better time management? Did you skip a prospecting day? Not enought time to prepare for that important meeting? Write it down!

_____

_____

_____

_____

$

Your Pipe: Did you generate any new pipe this week? Are you close? What actions do you need to take to get your prospect or the awesome discovery call you had into your pipe? Before you forget, write it down as a starting point for your focus next week.

_____

_____

_____

_____

**Your Profile**: Let's look at the numbers.

Is your forecast up to date?	☐ Yes ☐ No	
Does your activity dashboard look good?	☐ Yes ☐ No	
Did you generate new pipeline this week?	☐ Yes ☐ No	$ _____
Have you closed/won any deals this week?	☐ Yes ☐ No	$ _____

Work it! a modern-day sales planner

NOTES

My Focus THIS WEEK
3 STEPS TO MAKING MY QUOTA

1. Identify: What are my focus accounts for this week?
These can include net new prospects, accounts on life support, prospects that have gone dark or a recent discovery meeting that you desperately need to turn into pipeline.

1. _____
2. _____
3. _____
4. _____
5. _____

2. Action: What are my action items this week?
This is not your to-do list. These are tasks that will create real movement and generate action in your accounts. Is it sending a follow-up email or scheduling a follow-up meeting? Is it making an executive connection or mapping out a mutual close plan?

_____
_____
_____
_____
_____
_____

PRO TIP #1: Spread these action items out over the next five days.

PRO TIP #2: These are action items you can take into your 1:1 with your manager.

3. Reflect: What results do I need to manifest this week?
These are things that need to happen this week to feel good about your efforts. Which dashboards or activity metrics do you need to hit? What housekeeping tasks have you been assigned by your manager or team?

_____
_____
_____
_____
_____
_____

Work it! a modern-day sales planner

My Prospecting THIS WEEK
WORKSHEET

The hardest part about prospecting is finding the time. So now, let's make time. Record your *Target Prospects* for this week. Then look at the different types of *Prospecting Activity* you can engage in and pick the activity (or activities) you are going to dedicate time to this week. This exercise is not meant to replace your bulk outreach. Rather, it's the time you will dedicate to understanding your accounts and their business priorities.

PRO TIP #1: Don't cheat. You can repeat target prospects in the same week. But NEVER repeat the same combination in the same week!

PRO TIP #2: These are great action items and strategies you can take into your 1:1 with your SDR/BDR for your weekly planning session.

Sunday	Monday	Tuesday	Wednesday	Thursday	Friday	Saturday

Target Prospects	
Account	1
Account	2
Account	3
Account	4
Account	5

Prospecting Activity	
Research *(web articles, executive interviews, press releases, annual report, etc.)*	A
Organizational mapping *(including any partners)*	B
Draft call or email scripts	C
Schedule call or email blitz	D
Other	E

NOTES

_____

_____

_____

_____

_____

| Su | M | Tu | W | Th | F | Sa |

DAILY INTENTION

Date _____

My quota this month is _____

The non-negotiables for myself:

- ☐ Drink Water
- ☐ Move my body
- ☐ Be Awesome

Target prospect: _____

To make notable movement in my accounts, today I will: - List out activities from your weekly prospecting menu. - Act on the big things that will move the needle with your priority accounts.	At this time:
☐	
☐	
☐	
☐	
☐	
☐	
☐	
☐	
☐	
☐	
☐	
☐	
☐	
☐	
☐	
☐	
☐	
☐	
☐	
☐	
☐	
☐	

Work it! a modern-day sales planner

NOTES

Su M Tu W Th F Sa

DAILY INTENTION

Date _____

My quota this month is _____

The non-negotiables for myself:

☐ *Drink Water*

☐ *Move my body*

☐ *Be Awesome*

Target prospect:

To make notable movement in my accounts, today I will: - *List out activities from your weekly prospecting menu.* - *Act on the big things that will move the needle with your priority accounts.*	At this time:
☐	
☐	
☐	
☐	
☐	
☐	
☐	
☐	
☐	
☐	
☐	
☐	
☐	
☐	
☐	
☐	
☐	
☐	
☐	
☐	
☐	
☐	

Work it! a modern-day sales planner

NOTES

Su | M | Tu | W | Th | F | Sa

DAILY INTENTION

Date _____

My quota this month is _____

The non-negotiables for myself:

☐ *Drink Water*
☐ *Move my body*
☐ *Be Awesome*

Target prospect: _____

To make notable movement in my accounts, today I will: - *List out activities from your weekly prospecting menu.* - *Act on the big things that will move the needle with your priority accounts.*	At this time:
☐	
☐	
☐	
☐	
☐	
☐	
☐	
☐	
☐	
☐	
☐	
☐	
☐	
☐	
☐	
☐	
☐	
☐	
☐	
☐	
☐	
☐	

Work it! a modern-day sales planner

NOTES

Su	M	Tu	W	Th	F	Sa

DAILY INTENTION

Date _____

My quota this month is _____

The non-negotiables for myself:

- ☐ *Drink Water*
- ☐ *Move my body*
- ☐ *Be Awesome*

Target prospect:

To make notable movement in my accounts, today I will: - *List out activities from your weekly prospecting menu.* - *Act on the big things that will move the needle with your priority accounts.*	At this time:
☐	
☐	
☐	
☐	
☐	
☐	
☐	
☐	
☐	
☐	
☐	
☐	
☐	
☐	
☐	
☐	
☐	
☐	
☐	
☐	
☐	
☐	

Work it! a modern-day sales planner

NOTES

Su M Tu W Th F Sa   *Date* _____

DAILY INTENTION

My quota this month is _____

The non-negotiables for myself:

☐ *Drink Water*
☐ *Move my body*
☐ *Be Awesome*

Target prospect:

To make notable movement in my accounts, today I will: - *List out activities from your weekly prospecting menu.* - *Act on the big things that will move the needle with your priority accounts.*	At this time:
☐	
☐	
☐	
☐	
☐	
☐	
☐	
☐	
☐	
☐	
☐	
☐	
☐	
☐	
☐	
☐	
☐	
☐	
☐	
☐	
☐	
☐	

NOTES

Fri_YAY!

RECAP

+ **Your Peach**: What were you particularly proud of this week? Did you break into a new logo? Make a meaningful connection? Learn something new? Give a killer preso? Ink a deal? Write it down!

_____

_____

_____

_____

— **Your Pit**: Let's be real. Not everything goes as planned. What can you do better next week? Better time management? Did you skip a prospecting day? Not enought time to prepare for that important meeting? Write it down!

_____

_____

_____

_____

$ **Your Pipe**: Did you generate any new pipe this week? Are you close? What actions do you need to take to get your prospect or the awesome discovery call you had into your pipe? Before you forget, write it down as a starting point for your focus next week.

_____

_____

_____

_____

**Your Profile**: Let's look at the numbers.

Is your forecast up to date?	☐ Yes	☐ No	
Does your activity dashboard look good?	☐ Yes	☐ No	
Did you generate new pipeline this week?	☐ Yes	☐ No	$ _____
Have you closed/won any deals this week?	☐ Yes	☐ No	$ _____

Work it! a modern-day sales planner

NOTES

My Quarterly REVIEW

What's the one word you would use to describe
these last three months and your overall performance?

_____

What is my CLOSED/WON this quarter?   How does this map to my annual plan?

_____   _____

Take a moment now to reflect on your numbers and your performance.

☐ President's Club, here I come!

☐ Keeping calm and making progress.

☐ If I'm being honest, I need a better plan.

Did you crush it? If so, congratulations! Keep going and carry this momentum into next quarter. Did you lose sight of your goals? Why? What happened that got in your way? Write down all your blocks. Take a moment to reflect on what's really going on so that you can have the space and clarity to make any changes necessary before your next quarter begins.

_____

_____

_____

_____

_____

_____

Work it! a modern-day sales planner

Take a few moments now and quickly look through the completed pages of your journal, before you begin your next one. The way in which you have used, *or not used*, this journal can sometimes be a direct reflection on your individual habits, patterns, and overall performance. For example, is your pipeline a little light? Go back and take note of whether you spent enough time on your weekly prospecting worksheets. Have you skipped your daily planning and intentions and subsequently found that most of your days were reactive, not proactive? Are there some weeks when your journal engagement is lower than other weeks? These are all data points to consider when thinking about how to adjust your weekly and daily activity and to keep up your motivation for next quarter.

Remember, the more structure you have around your sales process, the better-and more consistent-your results will be. See you next quarter!

Congratulations! You did it.

Another quarter in the books.

Sales GLOSSARY

Account plan

A simple but powerful weapon in your sales tool kit (typically a document you create and build over time) that allows you to gather strategic insights and information about your prospect, the competitive landscape, and your overall sales approach and strategy. This document is also commonly called a DRD (Deal Review Document), walking deck, or another custom term your company has coined for their version of this deliverable.

ACV (Annual Contract Value)

Annual Contract Value is the value of a standard customer contract over a twelve-month period.

AE (Account Executive)

Account Executives are responsible for managing the entire sales effort associated with signing a deal with an organization's customer profile. Business-to-business organizations that sell software or technology products segment their target markets into small business, mid-market (or commercial), and enterprise. They group Account Executive talent in the same fashion.

ARR (Annual Recurring Revenue)

Annual Recurring Revenue is a key metric used by SaaS or subscription businesses that have Term subscription agreements, meaning there is a defined contract length. ARR is the value of the contracted recurring revenue components of your term subscriptions normalized to a one-year period.

B2B (Business-to-Business)

Business-to-Business refers to commerce between two businesses rather than to commerce between a business and an individual consumer. The dollar value of business-to-business transactions is significantly higher than business-to-consumer activity because businesses are more likely to purchase higher priced goods and services—and purchase more of them— than consumers are.

Work it! a modern-day sales planner

B2C (Business-to-Consumer)

Business-to-Consumer refers to commerce between a business and an individual consumer.

BDR (Business Development Representative)

Business Development Representative is also commonly referred to in most organizations as Sales Development Representative (SDR). This sales role focuses on generating qualified prospects using cold email, cold calling, social selling, and networking. BDR and SDR are traditionally the first step in a sales career and the number three role being recruited in technology sales today!

BHAG (Big Hairy Audacious Goal)

BHAG (pronounced BEE-hag) is a strategic business statement, similar to a vision statement, created to focus an organization on a single medium- to long-term organization-wide goal that is audacious, likely to be externally questionable, but not internally regarded as impossible.

Bluebird

We love bluebirds! A bluebird is a deal that lands unexpectedly in your lap, and closes in a relatively short time frame, for a quick win!

Bulk outreach

Bulk outreach is typically prospecting activity that is less personalized and is used to prospect at a much larger scale. While bulk outreach is more efficient to create and send, it should not replace more targeted and personalized outreach. Combining bulk outreach and more personalized outreach can have a higher conversion rate than bulk outreach alone.

CDI (Customer Data Infrastructure)

CDI is the new CRM. In order to focus on your customers, not your departmental divides, you need one shared source of truth. This requires the technical capability to collect every first-party interaction and integrate that data into the many tools your teams use.

CDP (Customer Data Platform)

A CDP is a type of packaged software that creates a persistent, unified customer database that is accessible to other systems. Data is pulled from multiple sources, cleaned, and combined to create a single customer profile. This structured data is then made available to other marketing systems.

CRM (Customer Relationship Management)

Customer relationship management is an approach to manage a company's interaction with current and potential customers. It uses data analysis about customers' history with a company to improve business relationships with customers, specifically focusing on customer retention, ultimately driving sales growth.

CSM (Customer Success Managers)

Customer Success Managers are relationship-focused client managers who align with clients post-sale to deliver goals for mutually beneficial outcomes.

CSR (Customer Service Representative)

Customer Service Representatives interact with customers to handle complaints, process orders, and provide information about an organization's products and services.

Enterprise sales

Enterprise selling, also known as complex sales in B2B companies, refers to the procurement of large contracts that typically involve long sales cycles, multiple decision-makers, and a higher level of risk than traditional sales. Enterprise sales are traditionally the last stop in a field sales career, and typically the launching pad for a transition into leadership. There is a standard career pathing in sales. First, you start as a Sales Development Representative (or SDR)— interestingly enough, the third most recruited role in technology today! A small business (commercial) or medium business (mid-market team) is often the first direct selling experience for a new sales rep. Finally, you graduate to enterprise.

Forecast

A forecast is the process of estimating future sales. Accurate sales forecasts enable companies to make informed business decisions and predict short- and long-term performance. Sales forecasting gives insight into how a company should manage its workforce, cashflow, and resources. Various sales teams within a company have their own sales forecast to manage, which then roll up to the company forecast.

IPO (Initial Public Offering)

An Initial Public Offering refers to the process of offering shares of a private corporation to the public in a new stock issuance. Tech IPOs multiplied at the height of the dot-com boom as startups without revenues rushed to list themselves on the stock market. After the recession following the 2008 financial crisis, IPOs ground to a halt and, for some years after, new listings were rare. More recently, much of the IPO buzz has moved to a focus on unicorns.

IT (Information Technology)

IT is technology involving the development, maintenance, and use of computer systems, software, and networks for the processing and distribution of data.

LOI (Letter of Intent)

The main purpose of a Letter of Intent (sometimes also referred to as a "Letter of Understanding" or "Memorandum of Understanding") is to facilitate the start of a business deal or project between the parties involved by identifying the key business and contractual understandings that will form the basis of the final agreement. LOIs are sometimes the path forward if there are significant delays in working through the final agreement. LOIs are not preferred in most cases given they require a significant amount of work and coordination across both companies when in reality your time is better spent on the due diligence required to work toward your final contract or Master Services Agreement (referred to as the MSA).

MAP (Mutual Action Plan)

A Mutual Action Plan is, quite literally, your map to closing a deal! It is a document that helps the account executive and prospective customer work together to find a mutually beneficial solution in a mutually beneficial timeframe.

MNDA (Mutual Non-Disclosure Agreement)

A Mutual Non-Disclosure Agreement is a non-disclosure agreement typically executed prior to engaging in conversations with an organization. An MNDA creates a confidential relationship between the parties, typically to protect any type of confidential and proprietary information or trade secrets—its distinguishing quality being its mutual intent, as its name suggests.

MSA (Master Services Agreement)

A Master Services Agreement, or MSA, is a contract reached between parties, in which the parties agree to most of the terms that will govern future transactions or future agreements.

NDA (Non-Disclosure Agreement)

A Non-Disclosure Agreement is typically executed prior to engaging in conversations with an organization. An NDA creates a confidential relationship between the parties, typically to protect any type of confidential and proprietary information or trade secrets.

OTE (On-Target Earnings)

OTE is a term often seen in job advertisements, especially for sales executives. While all commission plans are unique, often exceeding sales targets for a specific period results in higher commission rates.

POC (Proof of Concept)

POC is a short-term proof of concept, typically before a purchase is made. POCs can be conducted in either the form of a free or a paid POC.

Pull forward

A pull forward deal is typically used to reference a deal that is not forecasted for the current quarter. Sales managers frequently ask sales reps to look ahead at their forecast and look for any potential pull forward deals that can be closed in the current quarter.

Ramp

A company's sales ramp up time refers to the amount of time it takes a new salesperson to become fully productive from when they are first hired. Often, ramp time includes initial product training, sales coaching, and any and all onboarding that is part of the new-hire process.

ROI (Return on Investment)

Customer ROI (Return on Investment) is the primary reason why someone buys your SaaS product. Customers are making an investment by using their cash to pay for a software product on the assumption that it will deliver that value (if not more) back to the company in some form.

SA (Solutions Architect)

A Solutions Architect is the person in charge of leading the practice and introducing the overall technical vision for a particular solution.

SaaS (Software as a Service)

A software distribution model in which a third-party provider hosts applications and makes them available to customers over the Internet.

Sales QBR (Sales Quarterly Business Review)

A Sales QBR is an in-depth review of your sales pipeline and forecast that typically happens either quarterly or bi-annually.

Work it! a modern-day sales planner

SDR (Sales Development Representative)

A Sales Development Representative is also commonly referred to in most organizations as a Business Development Representative (BDR). This sales role focuses on generating qualified prospects using cold email, cold calling, social selling, and networking. SDR and BDR are traditionally the first step in a sales career and the number three role being recruited in technology sales today!

SE (Sales Engineer)

Sales Engineers are your best allies and partners-in-crime! They specialize in technologically and scientifically advanced products and sell these products or services, alongside the account executive, to businesses. They must have extensive knowledge of the parts and products they sell. Sales engineers may have extensive travel and may work additional hours to meet client needs or sales goals.

SLA (Service Level Agreement)

An SLA is a contract between a service provider and its internal or external customers that documents what services the provider will furnish and defines the service standards the provider is obligated to meet.

SMB (Small and Medium Business)

A small and midsize business is a business that, due to its size, has different IT requirements—and often faces different IT challenges—than large enterprises do, and whose IT resources (usually budget and staff) are often highly constrained.

SME (Subject Matter Expert)

A Subject Matter Expert, or domain expert, is a person who is an authority in a particular area or topic within an organization.

TCV (Total Contract Value)

Total Contract Value is the total value of a customer contract. TCV includes one-time and recurring revenue, but only the recurring revenue is specified in the contract.

Unicorn

A unicorn is a privately held startup company valued at over $1 billion. The term was coined in 2013 by venture capitalist Aileen Lee, choosing the mythical animal to represent the statistical rarity of such successful ventures.

Use case

A use case provides one or more scenarios for how a solution/system/product/service achieves a specific business goal. Very simply stated, a use case is a case study.

WYWYN (Why You, Why You Now)

How do you get someone you don't know to call you back? What can you say in the first thirty seconds of the call to get their attention? WYWYN is a prospecting tactic that is commonly used for effective outreach. It forces you to think very specifically about how to engage a prospect by answering the very specific questions—why you (the busy executive) must speak to me now!

YOY (Year Over Year)

A method of evaluating two or more measured events to compare the results at one period with those of a comparable period on an annualized basis. YOY comparisons are a popular and effective way to evaluate the financial performance of a company.

NOTES

NOTES

NOTES

NOTES

NOTES

NOTES

NOTES

NOTES

NOTES

NOTES

NOTES

TANIA ARAKELIAN DOUB accidentally stumbled into sales at the age of twenty six. Having landed in the right place at the right time—in her ideal sales environment!—Tania was among the top sales performers within twelve months. She has since worked at multiple high-growth SaaS companies, including e-Dialog, Tealium, PowerReviews, Segment, Yext—and now, Salesforce. She has made a career out of closing historically complex deals, advancing her companies' reputations and transforming how they do business. Tania has built her sales career while also balancing motherhood, the ongoing demands of a young family, and managing the general "you can have it all" prophecy that we are all constantly trying to fulfill.

Tania is also the author of **Work It, Girl! A modern-day career guide for women in sales**. The companion to this sales planner, **Work It, Girl!**, is the essential handbook for any modern-day woman navigating a career in technology sales. In her book, Tania compiles twenty years of her sales experience—job profiles, career trajectories, anecdotes, tips and tricks, and more—and has created the blueprint to a long and sustainable career for women in sales. Find it on www.Amazon.com or visit www.taniadoub.com.

Tania has received multiple sales awards and President's Club recognition over the years, but more importantly she has been rewarded by finding her voice—and her confidence—as a woman in sales. Tania lives in Boston, MA, with her husband, two young boys, and their goldendoodle, Lucky.

Author photo by Merissa Conley

Cover and journal design by Chiara Pennella

 FriesenPress

One Printers Way
Altona, MB R0G 0B0
Canada

www.friesenpress.com

ISBN
978-1-03-912628-2 (Hardcover)
978-1-03-912627-5 (Paperback)
978-1-03-912629-9 (eBook)

1.Business & Economics, Women in Business

Distributed to the trade by The Ingram Book Company

CPSIA information can be obtained
at www.ICGtesting.com
Printed in the USA
BVHW061542190722
642495BV00005B/259